How Things Move

Slow

Sarah Shannon

Heinemann
L I B R A R Y

www.heinemannlibrary.co.uk
Visit our website to find out more information about Heinemann Library books.

To order:
 Phone 44 (0) 1865 888066
 Send a fax to 44 (0) 1865 314091
 Visit the Heinemann Bookshop at www.heinemannlibrary.co.uk to browse our catalogue and order online.

Heinemann Library is an imprint of Capstone Global Library Limited, a company incorporated in England and Wales having its registered office at 7 Pilgrim Street, London, EC4V 6LB – Registered company number: 6695582

Heinemann is a registered trademark of Pearson Education Limited, under licence to Capstone Global Library Limited

Edited by Siân Smith, Rebecca Rissman, and Charlotte Guillain
Designed by Joanna Hinton-Malivoire
Picture research by Elizabeth Alexander
Production by Duncan Gilbert
Originated by Dot Gradations Ltd
Printed and bound in China by South China Printing Company Ltd

ISBN 978 0 431 19323 6
13 12 11 10 09
10 9 8 7 6 5 4 3 2 1

British Library Cataloguing in Publication Data
Shannon, Sarah
  Slow. - (How things move)
  1. Speed - Juvenile literature
  I. Title
  531.1'12

Acknowledgements
We would like to thank the following for permission to reproduce photographs: ©Alamy pp.**10**, **23 bottom** (Jeff Morgan heritage), **15** (Kim Karpeles), **7**, **23 top** (Martin Harvey), **14** (Robert Harding Picture Library Ltd); ©Capstone Global Library Ltd. pp.**13**, **18**, **23 middle** (Tudor Photography 2008); ©Corbis pp.**6** (David Sutherland), **19** (image100), **4** (Phil Schermeister), **5** (Steve Raymer); ©Digital Vision pp.**8**, **20**; ©iStockphoto.com p.**21** (Robert Churchill); ©Lonely Planet Images p.**12** (Eric Wheater); ©Photolibrary pp.**17** (Alix Minde/Photoalto), **9** (Cheryl Clegg/Index Stock Imagery), **16** (Geoff du Feu/Imagestate RM), **11** (Sebastien Boisse/ Photononstop)

Cover photograph of a tortoise reproduced with permission of ©Digital Vision. Back cover photograph of a snail reproduced with permission of ©Digital Vision.

Every effort has been made to contact copyright holders of material reproduced in this book. Any omissions will be rectified in subsequent printings if notice is given to the publishers.

Contents

Moving

Things can move in many ways.

4

Things can move from place to place.

Moving slowly

Some things move slowly.

Things that move slowly take a long
time to move from place to place.

A snail moves slowly.

A baby moves slowly.

A steamroller moves slowly.

A rowing boat moves slowly.

Pushes and pulls

A gentle pull can make something move slowly.

A gentle push can make something move slowly.

Moving slower

A dinghy is slower than a ship.

A bicycle is slower than a car.

As something slows down, it gets slower and slower.

As a swing slows down, it gets slower
and slower.

When you walk instead of run, you move more slowly.

When cars slow down, they move more slowly.

Slow things

Lots of things move slowly.

How slowly can you move?

What have you learned?

- Slow things take a long time to move from place to place.

- A gentle pull can make something move slowly.

- A gentle push can make something move slowly.

Picture glossary

pull make something move towards you

push make something move away from you

steamroller machine with large wheels that moves very slowly. It rolls over things to make them flat.

Index

Notes for parents and teachers
Before reading
Talk to the children about different ways of moving. Sometimes we move fast
and sometimes we move slowly. Ask the children when they move fast. (For example,
playing football, running races, riding a bike.) When do they move slowly? (For example,
in a crowded shop, in a queue.) Do some everyday actions, for example sitting down very
slowly, or writing on the board very slowly. Ask the children what you are doing and how
you are doing it.

After reading
• Tell children to work with a partner. One child moves something very slowly, for example a
  finger, a shoulder, a mouth. How quickly can the other partner work out what is moving?
• In the hall tell children to move in time to your drum beat. Start off with a brisk beat for
  fast walking and then slow right down. Can the children keep their balance and walk
  very slowly?
• Say the following poem with hand actions.
  "Slowly, slowly, very slowly creeps the garden snail.
  Slowly, slowly, very slowly up the garden rail.
  Quickly, quickly, very quickly like a little mouse,
  Quickly, quickly, very quickly, all around the house!"

MALPAS

MALPAS 7/7/18